6 six

7 seven

8 eight

9 nine

10 ten

Can you count?

2 ducks

5 apples

3 cars

8 butterflies

1 2 3 4 5

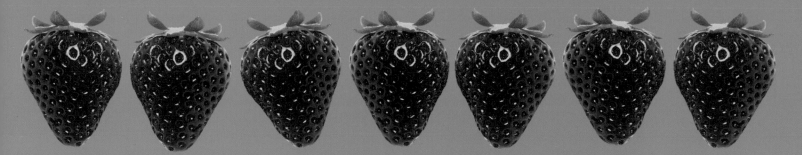

How many strawberries are there?

How many cupcakes can you see?

How many teddy bears are there?

6 7 8 9

Big and small

big

Small

Which animal is the biggest?

Which animal is the smallest?

A lot, a little, none

A lot   A little   None

More or less?

Are there more socks or more gloves?

Which cookie has the most candies?

11 eleven

12 twelve

13 thirteen

14 fourteen

15 fifteen

16 sixteen

17 seventeen

18 eighteen

19 nineteen

20 twenty

Can you add?

How many ladybugs are on the leaf?

How many ladybugs are not on the leaf?

How many ladybugs are there altogether?

How many red peppers are there?

How many green peppers are there?

How many peppers are there altogether?

30 thirty

40 forty

50 fifty

60 sixty

70 seventy

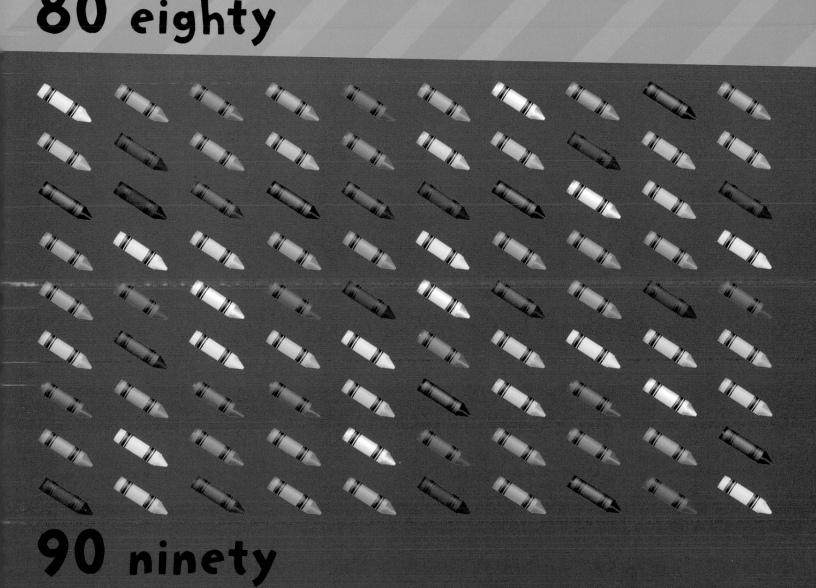

80 eighty

90 ninety

100 one hundred

How many pink candies can you see?

How many candies are round?